TRANSFORMING LOSS:
A DISCOVERY JOURNAL

Sally A. Smolen, MSN, PhD
and
Susan K. Zimmerman, MS

This is a companion book to TRANSFORMING LOSS: A DISCOVERY PROCESS and provides the reader a format for writing his/her way through the grief process.

This book uses references from TRANSFORMING LOSS and so it is recommended that the reader have copies of both books as they journal, though it is not essential.

The grief process shared in both books was discovered through the research, counseling, teaching, and personal journey of John M Schneider, PhD, Distinguished Professor Emeritus from Michigan State University's Colleges of Medicine, East Lansing, Michigan.

A more extensive description of his work can be found in FINDING MY WAY: FROM TRAUMA TO TRANSFORMATION: THE JOURNEY THROUGH LOSS AND GRIEF
by John M Schneider, PhD (Seasons Press, 2012).

We are indebted to the following people who helped in the creation of this companion book:

Kelly Rhoades, PhD
Shawn Johnson, PhD
Mary Elaine Kiener, PhD
Matthew Mulford
Gavin Witter
Christine Geith, PhD
Rita Marie Valade, PhD
Altair Boonraksa

ISBN # 0-9772980-1-9

INTEGRA PRESS
P.O. BOX 4005, East Lansing, MI 48826
www.integraonline.org

OTHER BOOKS

Books by John M. Schneider, PhD:

FINDING MY WAY From Trauma to Transformation: The Journey Through Loss and Grief
Seasons Press, 2012

TRANSFORMING LOSS: A Discovery Process with Susan K Zimmerman
INTEGRA Press, 2006

THE OVERDIAGNOSIS OF DEPRESSION: Recognizing Grief and Its Transformative
Potential
Seasons Press, 2000

GRIEF'S WISDOM: Quotes for Understanding the Transformative Process
Seasons Press, 2000

FINDING MY WAY: Healing and Transformation Through Loss and Grief
Seasons Press, 1994

STRESS, LOSS & GRIEF:Understanding Their Origins and Growth Potential
Aspen Systems, 1984

DEDICATION

We want to dedicate this journal
to the memory of
John Martin Schneider, PhD,
our colleague and mentor,
who, through years of working together,
became our cherished friend and brother.

His untimely death took his physical presence
from us much too soon
and we found ourselves
using methods he had taught us
as we struggled through our own grief.

Believing that death is not the end
of one's cherished relationships,
we want to affirm that
his spirit remains alive among us
and the mark he left on our hearts
will never grow dim.

TABLE OF CONTENTS

ILLUSTRATIONS

INTRODUCTION

This journal is a companion book to TRANSFORMING LOSS: A DISCOVERY PROCESS, a condensed version of a more comprehensive work by John M Schneider, PhD, which describes important elements of his theory of transformative grief.

Presented in the style of a journal, it serves as a companion guide to the book, offering a reflective approach for someone who desires to consider his/her process of grieving and work toward personal transformation.

The pages in this guide follow those in the companion book closely, though not in exact sequence.

TRANSFORMING LOSS begins with the concept of change, a constant reality in our human existence today. Whatever our life circumstances might be, there is no escaping the experience of change, and with change comes loss and its close companion grief. Whether we welcome it or dread it, nothing will protect us from experiencing the impact of change.

Discovery is a process with many meanings. To discover can mean to un-cover, to find, to unearth, to encounter, to break through, to see for the first time. Grief becomes a discovery process in which we find meaning by exploring the depth of our loss.

The poet Kahlil Gibran tells us,

> *"When you are sorrowful,*
> *look again into your heart*
> *and you shall see that in truth*
> *you are weeping for that which has been your delight."*

If someone (or something) has been our "delight," when it is lost, why would we not grieve?

CHANGE AS LOSS

Change disrupts how we relate to meaningful parts of our lives. It impacts the ways we experience, anticipate, and express ourselves. Typically, changes can be viewed as either one of two types: natural or disruptive.

Natural changes are those we experience during the years of growing up, with movement through our childhood and teen years, and then on to young adulthood, middle-age, and late adulthood.

Disruptive changes are those that we may not anticipate over the lifespan; such as divorce, job loss, or accidents, natural disasters, and illness of loved ones.

- When you think back over these years, what losses did you experience?

Childhood	Adolescence	Young Adulthood and Middle Age	Later Life and Aging Years

NATURAL CHANGES

- Which of these losses were associated with natural changes?

Natural Changes in Childhood	Natural Changes in Adolescence	Natural Changes in Young Adulthood and Middle Age	Natural Changes in Later Life and Aging Years

DISRUPTIVE CHANGES

When changes are disruptive, they may be "normal" at one age, but disruptive at another because they happened too soon or too late in our developmental process.

• What losses did you experience during these years that were associated with disruptive changes?

Disruptive Changes in Childhood	Disruptive Changes in Adolescence	Disruptive Changes in Young Adulthood and Middle Age	Disruptive Changes in Later Life and Aging Years

Grief is the healing mechanism that helps us make sense of the changes in our lives. It is a natural response to all types of change -- large or small -- those we view as positive as well as negative.

- Looking back at the changes and losses you have identified, which ones were associated with positive experiences? If any were positive, place an asterisk (*) next to them.

- What other positive changes come to mind as you reflect?

_____

_____

_____

_____

_____

_____

_____

_____

There is no despair so absolute
as that which comes with
the first moments of our first great sorrow,
when we have not yet known
what it is to have suffered and to be healed,
to have despaired and recovered hope.
George Eliot,
Adam Bede

- What made the experiences you identified positive rather than negative?

_____

_____

_____

_____

_____

_____

_____

- Some changes may be seen as positive but still have a somewhat negative impact. What may those be in your life?

_____

_____

_____

_____

_____

_____

LOSSES AND GAINS

Changes include losses <u>and</u> gains. Although TRANSFORMING LOSS focuses on the loss aspects, it may be helpful to pause and consider the gains which were part of the changes you have recalled.

Reviewing our life changes can bring a new perspective to how we view our personal history. Using a "lifeline diagram" can be useful in this process.

- Use the following diagram (or create one of your own) to illustrate these losses and gains.

- Place the gains above the lifeline and place the losses below the lifeline.

Table 4:1

Life Diagram Example

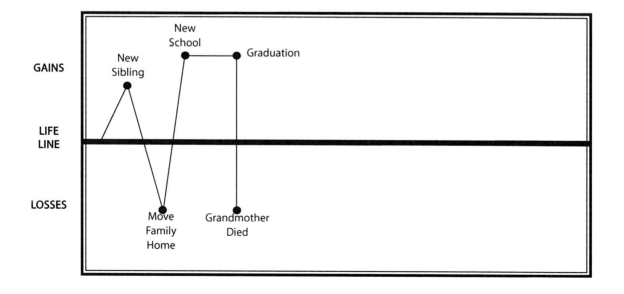

Table 4:2

Life Diagram

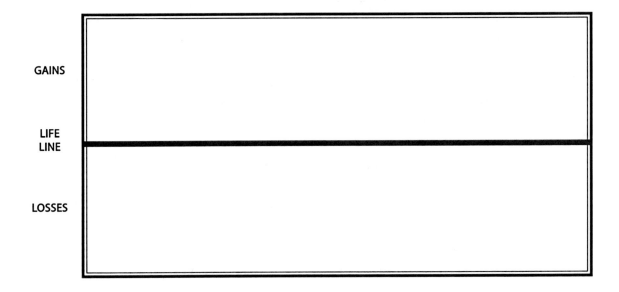

GAINS

LIFE
LINE

LOSSES

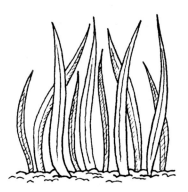

VALIDATION

Grief is a normal, human response to loss and someone who has good internal and external resources is generally able to work through the grief discovery process. A healthy grieving person with family, friends, or colleagues willing to offer support may not need professional help.

To be an effective helper, we need to:

- listen without judgment,

- encourage expression of deep thoughts, feelings, and validate (authenticate) the grieving person's unique experience – to let her/him know it is every bit as bad as it seems.

To validate another's experience, one needs to believe:

- the person is capable of handling reality,

- the person is doing the best s/he can at the present time,

- the person's way of coping is appropriate to the complexities and stressfulness of the loss, and

- s/he possesses the inner strength to make choices about her/his grief.

•   Consider the following questions and write about them in the space that follows:

_____

_____

_____

_____

_____

_____

•   Who can you identify as persons in your life who have been supportive in these ways?

_____

_____

_____

_____

_____

_____

- Have you asked others for help and support, and if yes, how did they respond?

_____

_____

_____

_____

_____

_____

_____

Table 5:1

PRINCIPLES OF VALIDATION

★ Commit to Empowering the Best Self
>   Believe in the inherent worth, dignity and integrity of all individuals
>   Believe in an individual's ability to rise to the occasion
>   Believe that there is more to people than what "meets the eye"

★ Appreciate the Moment & the Journey
>   Live the moment fully
>   Savor the journey and the process
>   Honor sacredness

★ Witness the Moment & the Process
>   Hold hope
>   Be present at significant times
>   Share in an ongoing story

★ Be Gentle, with Honesty & Find Abiding Truths
>   Be sensitive to communication dilemmas
>   Commit to gentleness of the moment and truth of the process

★ Suspend Judgment
>   Help to create emotional & spiritual safety
>   Know & respect your own values
>   Acknowledge differing viewpoints
>   Temporarily set aside perspectives that are not helpful in the moment

• Looking at the principles of validation on Table 5:1 as described, how is your experience of help from others reflected there?

_____

_____

_____

_____

_____

_____

_____

• Which of these principles or key points were missing in your experience?

_____

_____

_____

_____

_____

_____

_____

Many people, with good external support, are able to work through their grief process without professional help. At the same time, it often helps to find a health professional who can validate our experiences.

• If you felt the need for professional help, were you able to find someone with validating skills? How would you describe this experience?

_____

_____

_____

_____

_____

_____

_____

Even when professional resources are identified, it is important to look for these validation principles in your interactions with them.

**For further information on Validation, see pages 21-23 in "Transforming Loss: A Discovery Process"

TRANSFORMATIVE GRIEF

Professor John M. Schneider created the theory of transformative grief after many years of teaching, research, and counseling people with significant losses. He believed grieving people could hope for more than acceptance of their losses. This inspired him to develop an approach that explores the varied aspects of grief and taps its potential for transformation.

This existential theory includes all types of loss, death-related and non-death-related, through the lens of discovery, and invites a grieving person to enter the process by asking three questions: What is Lost? What is Left? What is Possible?

I consider grief to be composed of themes, or phases,
which occur in the context of a three-step discovery sequence:

What is lost?
What is left?
What is possible?
John M Schneider, PhD

WHAT IS LOST?

This first question invites us to sort out what actually is lost.
How deep is it?
How much has this impacted our lives?
How much of life has changed?
What is missing and no longer part of our lives?
What is no longer possible?

- Jot down what comes to mind with these questions.

What is Lost?

- Grief often begins with shock and we ask ourselves: Has this really happened? Is this real or a dream?

- If you have had moments when you felt you were walking around in a daze, how would you describe these moments?

_____

_____

_____

_____

_____

_____

_____

_____

What is Lost?

- Sometimes, putting these moments into words is difficult. If this is true for you, are there images that can help you describe them?

- Use this space for diagrams, drawings, etc. - add colors or shapes to express your feelings.

What is Lost?

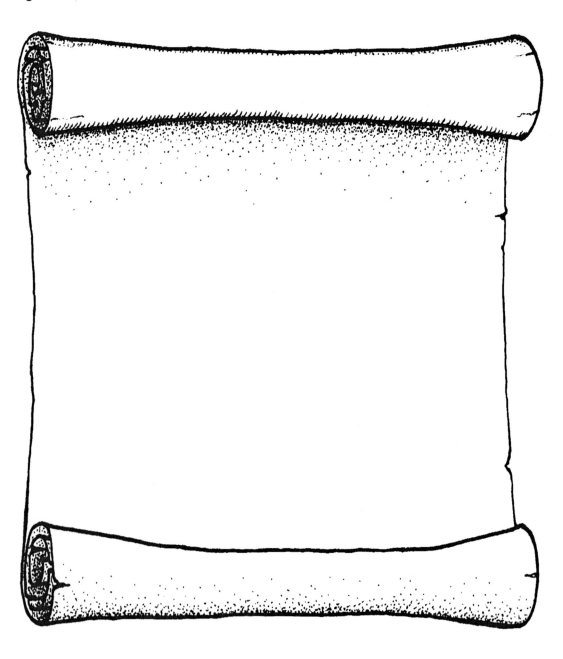

- What insights come from your images?

_____

_____

_____

_____

_____

_____

_____

_____

People do not die for us immediately,
but remain bathed in a sort of aura of life...
It is as if they were traveling abroad.
Marcel Proust
Remembrance of Things Past

What is Lost?

- Sometimes these moments can be expressed in music. If this is true for you, what song or music composition comes to mind?

_____

_____

_____

_____

_____

_____

_____

_____

- What favorite quotes, if any, help express these moments?

_____

_____

_____

_____

_____

_____

_____

_____

What is Lost?

- What other ways have you found helpful to express these moments?

_____

_____

_____

_____

_____

_____

_____

Addressing our losses as we try to cope with what we have lost can feel as if we are playing a game of ping-pong -- we go back-and-forth between the need to protect ourselves from being overwhelmed to allowing the full impact of what is lost into our awareness.

- How do you express the extremes you feel?

_____

_____

_____

_____

_____

_____

_____

What is Lost?

- If you could place your coping moments on a continuum, where would they fall?

[_____]

1   2   3   4   5
protect self   allow impact

- What are others saying to you as you try to cope?

_____

_____

_____

_____

_____

_____

_____

_____

_____

_____

What is Lost?

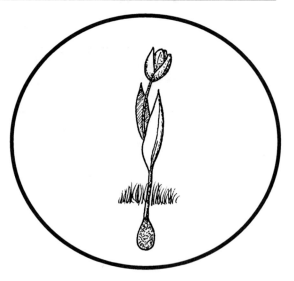

- How are others helping or blocking your awareness of what is lost?

_____

_____

_____

_____

_____

_____

- What are you saying to yourself to help and/or block your awareness of what is lost?

_____

_____

_____

_____

_____

_____

_____

_____

_____

_____

What is Lost?

VARIETIES OF LOSS

A key factor to understanding our grief is the degree of <u>attachment</u> that we had for that which is lost.

The attachment need not be a positive one – it may even have been negative or conflicted. This is why some people grieve the very person or thing they disliked.

• What losses are you grieving where there was deep attachment? List and describe them here:
1.
2.
3.
4.
5.
6.
7.
8.
9.
10.

Another factor that is important to understanding our grief is whether the loss was anticipated or unexpected.

Go back through the above list and mark beside each item: U (unanticipated) or A (anticipated) or B (both).

Grief will also differ depending on the degree of choice we had in the loss.

•   Describe any element of choice you had in your loss.

_____

_____

_____

_____

_____

_____

_____

•   Describe any lack of choice you had in your loss.

_____

_____

_____

_____

_____

_____

_____

Some losses are fairly obvious and typically understood by society as a loss. Others are more difficult to recognize. This can also be an important factor in our grieving.

• Based on your experience you may want to comment here.

_____

_____

_____

_____

_____

_____

_____

_____

Table 8:1

VARIETIES OF LOSS

OBVIOUS LOSSES

death of a spouse, partner, loved one
death of a child
stillbirth
miscarriage
divorce
separation
illness
chronic illness
disability

theft
destruction of property
moving
buying/selling valued objects

loss of a dream
relationship ending

job layoff
job change

COLLECTIVE LOSSES

natural disaster
loss of shelter, food or safety

ORGANIZATIONAL LOSSES

company closing
company re-organization
business failure

LOSS AS PART OF CHANGE

maturation
relationship maturation
aging
loss of memory

weaning
puberty changes
leaving home
child leaving home
starting school

POSITIVE EVENTS

being in love
marriage
birth of a child

wealth
fame
winning a prize

mastering a new skill
forming a new relationship
graduating or finishing school
ending therapy

job promotion
business success
project completion
retirement

- Looking at the table of losses included here, what examples of your experiences did you not recognize as losses before now?

1.
2.
3.
4.
5.
6.
7.
8.
9.
10.

- If you could add something to this list, what would it be?

- Add any of these to the list or create your own list here:

_____

_____

_____

_____

_____

_____

_____

_____

Sorrow was like the wind. It came in gusts.
Marjorie Kinnan Rawlings,
South Moon Under

INTERNAL ASPECTS OF LOSS

Losses can challenge what gives our life meaning. We may lose a sense of connection to anything or anyone.

- As you reflect on your values, priorities and things that are essential, can you name what seems to be essential to your being alive?

- What are the "connections" you consider essential?

- Has your experience of loss challenged any of these?

- Reflect for a moment on the questions above and write down your responses in the space below:

It is obvious that our experience of spiritual wholeness can be disrupted when our belief system is challenged. Validating spiritual losses is important if we are to grieve them. Our will to live determines what it takes for us to survive. Every significant loss evokes spiritual questions.

- Sometimes during grief's darkest hour, we find ourselves asking, "Is there enough left for me to keep going?" If you have experienced this, reflect on it here.

_____

_____

_____

_____

_____

_____

_____

- Spiritual issues are core issues. Sometimes in grief we think "Why me?" or "What did I do to deserve this?"

- How does this relate to your experience?

_____

_____

_____

_____

_____

_____

- In grief's dark hour we may wonder "What's the point of living now?" If you have had similar thoughts or feelings, reflect on this.

_____

_____

_____

_____

_____

_____

_____

- It can be helpful to express these sentiments to someone. Have you done this? Why or why not?

_____

_____

_____

_____

_____

_____

_____

_____

- How have others responded?

_____

_____

_____

_____

_____

_____

- Share any additional thoughts or feelings that have surfaced during this phase of your grief

_____

_____

_____

_____

_____

_____

_____

The delicate and infirm go for sympathy,
not to the well and buoyant,
but to those who have suffered like themselves.
Catharine Esther Beecher,
Woman Suffrage & Woman's
Professions

WHAT IS LEFT?

Once we have explored the extent of our loss and discovered we can go on, healing can begin. During this time, we look for what is left or what remains. We remember what we have lost and we look for what else is meaningful in our lives --- what was not lost.

- Does enough remain? Is enough recoverable?

- If not, then what?

- Is it the end of life as we once knew it?

- Is becoming a permanent victim of my circumstances all I can be?

- What thoughts come to your mind as you read this description of the phase of loss?

- How would you answer the above questions now?

What is Left?

Occasionally a grieving person or family is not able to move beyond their experience of what is lost?
They remain at this point in their grieving process.

• If you have encountered anyone like this, what lessons might you find in this?

What is Left?

_____

_____

_____

_____

_____

_____

_____

_____

_____

_____

_____

_____

_____

There is a land of the living
and a land of the dead
and the bridge is love,
the only survival,
the only meaning.
Thornton Wilder
The Bridge Of San Luis Rey

To choose ways to grow, we need to take risks and move beyond accepting and adjusting to our losses. We take on tasks that include the discovery of life's potentials. Often people experience something like a rite of passage. They find or create rituals that give witness to their growth process.

- How have you found or created ways to express your commitment to growth? Please describe in words or images.

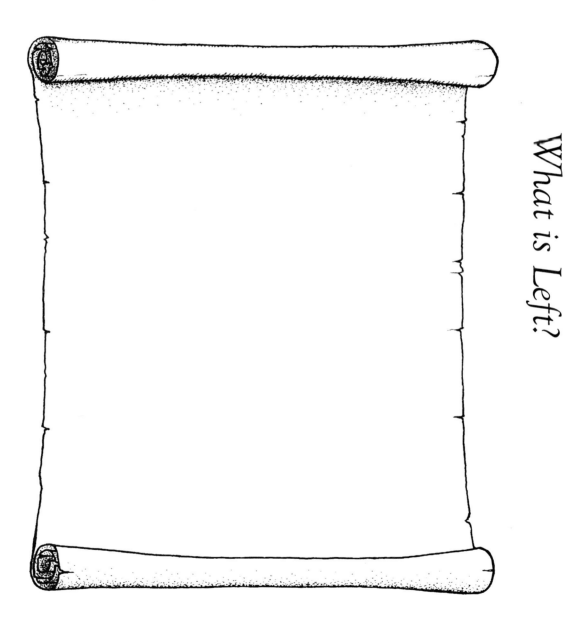

What is Left?

The process of integrating loss into the fabric of life can be the hardest part of grief, for it involves rebuilding and restoration. It is helpful when we can find forgiveness and move beyond the role of victim. This is the time when we take on the "tasks of grief." This is the place in grief that is work.

- What words or phrases would you use to describe your "tasks of grief"?

_____

_____

_____

_____

_____

_____

_____

_____

_____

What is Left?

- Are there images that can help you describe this?

- Use this space for diagrams, drawings, etc. - add colors or shapes to express your feelings.

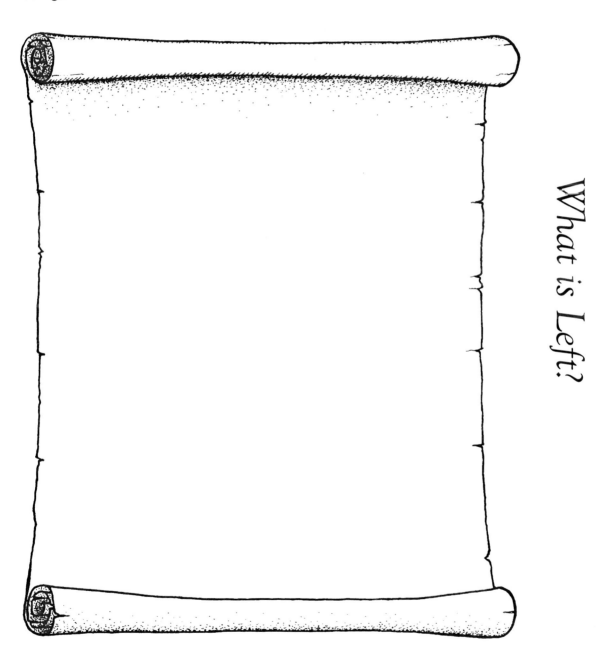

What is Left?

- What insights come from your images?

_____

_____

_____

_____

_____

_____

_____

- What song or music composition comes to mind that expresses this for you?

_____

_____

_____

_____

_____

_____

What is Left?

• What favorite quotes, if any, help express this time?

_____

_____

_____

_____

_____

_____

_____

_____

• What other ways have you found helpful to express these moments?

_____

_____

_____

_____

_____

_____

What is Left?

> We could never learn to be brave and patient,
> if there were only joy in the world.
> Helen Keller
> Atlantic

WHAT IS POSSIBLE?

Time spent with this question involves moving away from a focus on limitations to admitting a range of new and ever-widening possibilities. It is often a time of relinquishing old patterns. It may include the loss of others who were supportive during the early time of grief, but now are frightened or mystified by our desire to move on.

- When did your attitude change or begin to change?

What is Possible?

Sometimes as we move through grief, we may find that relationships with others have changed.

• What relationships that were initially supportive have "disappeared" now?

_____

_____

_____

_____

_____

_____

_____

_____

• What new relationships have emerged?

_____

_____

_____

_____

_____

_____

_____

What is Possible?

- Describe how you have experienced any of this third discovery of grief or if you have not, can you see some beginning steps?

_____

_____

_____

_____

_____

_____

What is Possible?

> *Die when I may,*
> *I want it said of me*
> *by those who knew me best,*
> *that I always plucked a thistle*
> *and planted a flower*
> *where I thought the flower would grow.*
> Abraham Lincoln

You can use this space to describe these experiences:

- Images, diagrams or drawings

- Color or shapes

- Song titles or words

- Quotations

What is Possible?

The central focus of this time is reformulation -- focus on new things or old things with a "new eye." Self-empowerment also becomes pivotal to being a survivor. This time addresses the possibilities created out of this loss -- not its limits, nor simply ways to continue in spite of the loss. In other words, what can happen because of the loss.

•   How Is this happening or not taking place in your experience now?

_____

_____

_____

_____

_____

_____

_____

_____

_____

•   Envision how this could happen for you?

_____

_____

_____

_____

_____

_____

_____

What is Possible?

At this moment in the discovery process we are not yet what we will become, but we are on the way. In this discovery, we must abandon our search for the ONE right answer --- or the BEST way. We are being freed from a focus on limitations to envision opportunities.

• Describe any times you may have found yourself hesitating to try something because it might not be right?

_____

_____

_____

_____

_____

_____

_____

• How is your life characterized by limits or opportunities?

_____

_____

_____

_____

_____

_____

_____

What is Possible?

Dreams can be another source of information and learning. They can help us move through our grief.

• What is happening in your sleep dreams?	• What is happening in your day dreams?

What is Possible?

•   How might you imagine turning any of these dreams into reality?

_____

_____

_____

_____

_____

_____

_____

_____

_____

_____

_____

TRANSFORMATIVE GRIEF

The word "transformation" means a significant alteration in the form of something -- moving across or beyond the old form to something unknown or unknowable before the change began. It is opening to a larger reality. We sense discontinuity as we go through any major life transition. That sense of discontinuity is what we often call grief.

- How does this description resonate with your experience?

Transformative Grief

An ongoing process of renewal and discovery is often part of this phase.

•   How have you experienced it, or not?

Transformative Grief

You can use this space to describe these experiences:

- Images, diagrams or drawings

- Color or shapes

- Song titles or words

- Quotations

Transformative Grief

- Less fear and resistance also can be part of this new growth.

- How have you experienced this? Or how not?

_____

_____

_____

_____

_____

_____

_____

_____

_____

_____

_____

_____

_____

_____

_____

_____

_____

_____

Transformative Grief

GRIEF DIFFERS FROM DEPRESSION

It is not uncommon for a grieving person to speak of feeling "depressed," and grief can sometimes be accompanied by (or become) clinical depression; but it is important to be able to distinguish the two states. The word "grieving" suggests it is possible to know why one feels sad, for grief is directly related to a tangible loss of connection with someone or something we cherish. Clinical depression, on the other hand, is a state of disconnection, an imbalance that makes it all-but-impossible to function fully. Although the two emotional states are too often confused, there are key differences between them. These key differences and typical behaviors are not intended to be used as a comprehensive clinical assessment, but they may be indicators of the need for professional help.

* Looking at the key differences listed in Table 13:1, which ones describe your experience?

_____

_____

_____

_____

_____

Table 13:1

TYPICAL BEHAVIORS OF GRIEF & DEPRESSION

Grieving (but not depressed) people may:
- find dreams helpful
- fear they are going crazy
- admit their feelings scare them
- say "I feel depressed"
- never forget who or what they lost
- respond to nurturance and support
- find the courage to forgive and let go
- admit they need help
- be open to every consequence of a loss
- be motivated to create new meaning in their lives
- hope that things might get better someday
- need validation that things are as bad as they seem
- eventually be able to realize their wholeness comes out of that grief
- say, "If I continue to feel this way, I'm not sure life is worth living."
- "look good" six months after a loss even when they still don't feel good
- choose not to go back to life before the loss occurred if it means giving up the growth resulting from their grief

Depressed people may:

- be unable to forgive
- be at risk for suicide
- pray only for deliverance, not for strength
- find their dreams repetitive and disturbing
- refuse to talk about or acknowledge that loss
- be unable to cry or unable to stop crying
- avoid their feelings or constantly live in them
- believe nobody cares and have developed ways to prove it
- believe perfection is possible and that forgiveness is impossible
- be unable to tolerate the good times and rain on other people's parades
- dislike being touched or can never get enough touching (sex)

Both grieving <u>and</u> depressed people may:

- lose or gain weight
- have trouble sleeping
- feel tired and exhausted
- not want to be hurt again
- avoid pleasurable activities

Mark those which describe your experience and indicate if they fall into one column or both.

- Describe your experience with those that fall in both columns.

_____

_____

_____

_____

_____

_____

_____

_____

**For further information on Grief & Depression comparison see pages 24 -30 in "Transforming Loss: A Discovery Process".

GRIEF IS A HOLISTIC PROCESS

Grief pervades our entire being following a significant loss and involves all five dimensions of ourselves: the ways we act (behavioral), how we think (cognitive), the feelings we have (emotional), the responses of our body (physical), and the meaning and values we have (spiritual). We may be profoundly aware of this or it may be less apparent – both to us as well as to others around us.

The three themes of grief do not necessarily occur in sequence. At times, they will overlap and complement each other and may even contradict each other.

- When you consider the first theme of grief --- WHAT IS LOST? How has your loss impacted these five dimensions of yourself?

_____

_____

_____

_____

_____

_____

_____

_____

- Are you aware of the impact on one dimension more than another?

- If so, which dimension has been impacted most and how?

_____

_____

_____

_____

_____

_____

_____

_____

_____

- What, if any dimension, has NOT been impacted?

_____

_____

_____

_____

_____

_____

_____

- When you consider the second theme of grief --- WHAT IS LEFT? How has your loss impacted these five dimensions of yourself?

_____

_____

_____

_____

_____

_____

_____

_____

- Are you aware of the impact on one dimension more than another?

- If so, which dimension has been impacted most and how?

_____

_____

_____

_____

_____

_____

_____

_____

- What, if any, dimension has NOT been impacted?

_____

_____

_____

_____

_____

_____

_____

_____

- When you consider the third theme of grief --- WHAT IS POSSIBLE---how has your loss impacted these five dimensions of yourself?

_____

_____

_____

_____

_____

_____

_____

_____

- Are you aware of the impact on one dimension more than another?

- If so, which dimension has been impacted most and how?

_____

_____

_____

_____

_____

_____

_____

_____

- What if any dimension has NOT been impacted?

_____

_____

_____

_____

_____

_____

_____

_____

_____

MODES OF HEALING --
MASCULINE AND FEMININE

Men and women often misunderstand each other's grieving processes. As a rule, though not always, men want to put the loss behind them and to cope by being productive – washing the car, mowing the lawn, making household repairs, for example. As a rule, though not always, women tend to be open and inclusive in expressing their loss -- sharing their feelings, crying tears, embracing each other, for example.

If we are not careful, we can too easily misinterpret these behaviors to mean men are not grieving and women are grieving too much. In reality, both women and men are grieving. It is their emphasis that demonstrates different aspects of the grieving process.

• How have you observed differences among men and women as they grieve?

• How have these behaviors been similar or different from your own?

_____
_____
_____
_____
_____
_____
_____
_____
_____
_____
_____
_____

- If you encountered any misinterpretations by others of your grieving behaviors, describe that experience here.

You can use this space to describe these experiences:

- Images, diagrams or drawings

- Color or shapes

- Song titles or words

- Quotations

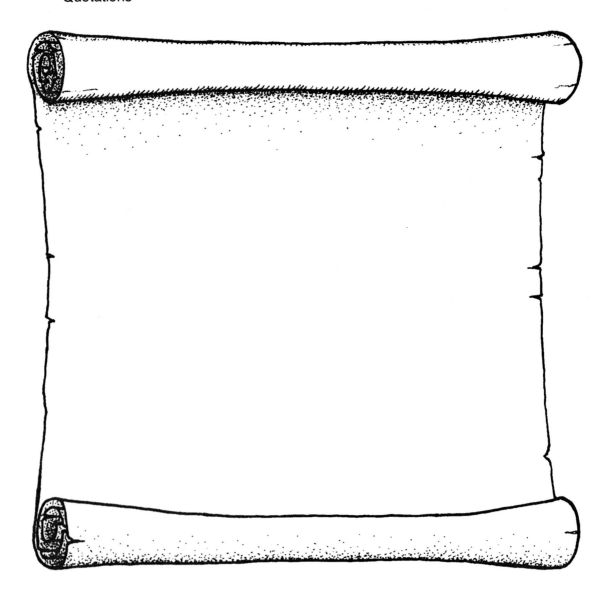

DISCOVERIES AND CHOICES, NOT STAGES AND PHASES

Dr. Elizabeth Kubler-Ross's research and writing ON DEATH AND DYING is highly regarded as pioneer work in the study of loss and grief. Nearly every adult can state the five psychological states she proposed as the stages of grief: denial, anger, bargaining, depression, and acceptance. Unfortunately, her work with its primary focus on emotional stages has been misunderstood and misapplied for a long time.

What is too often overlooked is that her study involved dying patients and she was doing research and writing at a time when people were not talking about death. It was very common then for a family to ask the physician and health care personnel to refrain from telling the patient s/he was dying and, just as often, patients would ask that their families not be told their terminal diagnosis. It was this societal context that made her study so remarkable.

Her five stages were not intended to be an inflexible sequence that one must follow in order to grieve properly. She did not intend that any difference was to be considered complicated grief and required professional help. Years of research with death-related loss and non-death-related loss have expanded our concepts beyond what was initially proposed by Kubler-Ross in the 1960s. We know so much more now.

- Have you found yourself wondering about these five stages of grief?

- Have you ever asked yourself or others if you are grieving "properly"?

- Have you encountered others who question your process of grief?

- Reflect on these questions and write your responses in the space below.

_____

_____

_____

_____

_____

_____

_____

_____

_____

_____

_____

_____

_____

_____

IMPORTANT FACTS ABOUT GRIEF

1. The natural outcome of experiencing a significant loss is a process of grieving.

2. Grief is a healing process.

3. The loss of any significant attachment is a threat to all significant attachments, including our own life.

4. We can't take in a loss all at one time.

5. The ways we have dealt with previous changes in our lives will affect our reactions to current and future losses.

6. We don't "get over" a significant loss, but we can move on.

- As you consider these facts about grief, how is your experience reflected in them?

_____

_____

_____

_____

_____

_____

_____

_____

- Which facts resonate with your experience?

_____

_____

_____

_____

_____

_____

When something rotten like this happens,
then you have your choice.
You start to really be alive, or you start to die.
That's all.
James Agee
A Death In The Family

- What might be questions in-between the lines of these facts that arise within you?

- Describe and explain.

_____

_____

_____

_____

_____

_____

_____

- Reflect further on these facts.

_____

_____

_____

_____

_____

_____

_____

_____

GRIEF AND SOCIETY

It is a myth of modern society that success in relationships, individual accomplishments, technology, fame, wealth, or knowledge can eliminate the necessity of grieving. Occasionally, we discard that myth in the process of surviving wars and natural disasters when collective grieving takes place. Our evening newscasts often feature human interest stories of people who put aside their personal agendas to fight, shelter, shovel, and sandbag for collective survival. These experiences almost always have a profound impact on those involved.

- If you ever survived an experience of a natural disaster, like a tornado or a flood, or something similar, what did you learn about yourself, and possibly about others?

_____

_____

_____

_____

_____

_____

_____

_____

_____

_____

FACING OUR GREATEST FEARS CAN BE LIBERATING

We can place some of our smaller fears in a larger context when we have faced our greatest fears --- dying, loneliness, helplessness, loss of meaning and purpose --- that can result from facing a significant loss.

- What might the "greatest fear" be for you?

_____

_____

_____

_____

_____

_____

- Have you dealt with it or what would it take for you to face it?

_____

_____

_____

_____

_____

_____

FIRST THE DARKNESS,
THEN THE LIGHT

There is a belief that it is possible to go through life without really having to come to grips with reality. These beliefs generally involve one of three forms of selective consciousness: emphasis on the survival capacity of human nature; freedom from responsibility that comes from seeing oneself as a victim; the notion that people always have choices, including the choice to avoid suffering. People use this selective awareness to create false alternatives to experiencing loss and grief.

• What might be any of these beliefs?

_____

_____

_____

_____

_____

_____

• What beliefs in your life might be similar?

_____

_____

_____

_____

_____

•   What led you to embrace these beliefs?

_____

_____

_____

_____

_____

_____

_____

_____

•   Have any of these led you to create false alternatives?

_____

_____

_____

_____

_____

_____

• How are these alternatives working for you, or not?

To find deeper meaning in life, it is important to consciously embrace and address three aspects of reality - challenges which are part of a larger process of effective grieving:
(a) Suffering exists and cannot be avoided without paying an even greater price;
(b) When suffering is validated, healing results;
(c) Suffering and healing renew possibilities for love and joy.

- Have you found yourself avoiding the suffering involved in grieving a loss? Please explain.

_____

_____

_____

_____

_____

_____

_____

_____

_____

- What, if any, "even greater price" have you experienced from this?

_____

_____

_____

_____

- How did this "greater price" find expression?

_____

_____

_____

_____

- Have you experienced the healing that comes with validation? Describe fully.

_____

_____

_____

_____

Whether we share our loss with others or not, it is through discovering the interweaving of our life experiences with loss that we find the universal threads that give hope --- the threads which tell us that by fully facing what we experience, we can know what we have lost, what we have left, and what is possible.

• As you address the challenges in your grieving, describe any "threads that give hope" that you have discovered.

• If there is a special shape or form to these "threads", please describe here.

Loss happens to everyone who makes connections. We create and maintain continuing bonds with those we love who have died. We are all connected to each other. The experience of grief is unique to each individual, but we are never alone.

- What are the connections and continuing bonds in your life?

_____

_____

_____

_____

_____

_____

_____

_____

_____

- At this moment, does your experience of grief feel more individual than connected with others? And if so, explain it here.

_____

_____

_____

_____

_____

- What might help you experience more connectedness with others?

_____

_____

_____

_____

_____

Opportunities for recovery and transformation come when we believe in ourselves. Grieving and recovery may not be easy, but they can be joyful.

- Looking at the description of these experiences in Table 20:1, reflect and write down your thoughts and feelings.

_____

_____

_____

_____

_____

_____

_____

_____

_____

_____

Table 20:1

EXPERIENCES FOR RECOVERY

<u>These things can help us move through the process of grieving and recovery</u>:

❖ feeling cared for

❖ being validated for the reality of the loss

❖ seeking facilitative environments

❖ finding places of sanctuary

❖ building therapeutic communities

❖ including play & humor

❖ creating rituals of recognition & commemoration

❖ testing our limits

❖ forgiving & being forgiven

❖ learning new means of creative expression while grieving

❖ recognizing our strengths in surviving & moving through the process

- Which of these have been part of your experience?

List	Comments
1.	
2.	
3.	
4.	
5.	
6.	
7.	
8.	
9.	
10.	

- Which ones have **NOT**?

List	Comments
1.	
2.	
3.	
4.	
5.	
6.	
7.	
8.	
9.	
10.	

- Which ones would you want to pursue?

List	Comments
1.	
2.	
3.	
4.	
5.	
6.	
7.	
8.	
9.	
10.	

NEW POSSIBILITIES

Transforming loss into a fuller life is a gift. When we grow from a loss, we create a deeper, more enduring sense of hope that the destructive energies in our world can be transformed.

The gift of knowing we can change means other transformations are also possible. This gift means we can find hope in the face of despair. This gift means we can remain open to what lies ahead and even beyond. This gift means there are discoveries that can truly enrich our lives beyond anything we might have dreamed could be.

Transforming loss allows us to discover new ways to relate, understand, create and commit ourselves to an ongoing process of renewal and discovery. Our experience of the grieving process can empower us to a greater understanding of ourselves and of others when we are suffering and, ultimately, help us create a more accepting and caring world.

• Reaching this point, what are the ways you might describe this moment for yourself?

_____

_____

_____

_____

_____

_____

_____

_____

_____

_____

Again you can use this space to describe this experience:

- Images, diagrams or drawings

- Color or shapes

- Song titles or words

- Quotations

- Maybe even a dance comes to mind

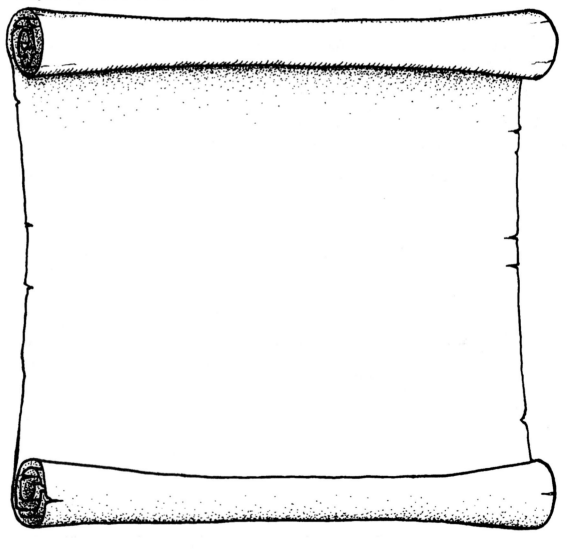

Once you have completed this guide, you may uncover the need to refer back to it at times in the future. You may want to add new reflections or adapt older ones, you may also discover the need to connect with and talk to a professional grief counselor to continue the exploration of what this loss means to you.

However you find yourself, use this guide to help you move toward transformation.

Transformations astonish and fascinate.
They tap hope in the face of despair.
Transformations are restorations of the human spirit,
the throwing off of the burden of fear, pain and loneliness.
John M. Schneider, PhD

MEET THE AUTHORS

Sally A. Smolen, MSN, PhD

Sally is a Transformative Grief Specialist, a certification earned through graduate studies with Dr. John M. Schneider and Susan K. Zimmerman.

A dedicated health professional, she has an extensive background in the healing profession which includes nursing, clinical psychology, adult education, music and spirituality. Her special interests focus on varied loss and grief issues occurring in death-and non-death-related moments across the life span.

Sally integrates Schneider's concepts of Transformative Grief Theory when she meets with individuals and groups through her private practice, MERCY WORKS.

Susan K. Zimmerman, M.S.

Susan collaborated with John M. Schneider, PhD on the book "Transforming Loss: A Discovery Process," and together they co-founded INTEGRA: The Association of Grief and Loss.

Currently she is coaching individuals and consulting with organizations that are dealing with major transition. She has worked for over 20 years leading support groups, creating classes, and working with people dealing with loss and change.

A recognized speaker, she coaches and consults through Passages Transition Center where she now devotes full-time after retiring from Michigan State University.

Integra's logo or wordmark incorporates several images. At the upper left, a teardrop transforms into a flower bud. Representing sadness associated with the grieving process, the teardrop flows into the flower bud denoting a new beginning for the grieving individual. The butterfly is next, symbolizing change while also forming the leaves of the flower. Those leaves attach to the stem emanating from the seed below, portraying growth and a continuation of healing through grief, also forming the letter 'I' at the start of 'Integra'.

INTEGRA is dedicated to sharing the mission and value of transformative grief. Our basic philosophy is that loss and grief– when fully experienced – can positively transform lives.

We know that:

❖ Grieving is a normal process

❖ Grief extends beyond coping, adjustment and survival

❖ Validating grief is essential for healing

❖ Effective grieving integrates mind, body, and spirit

❖ Grief differs from depression

❖ Grief, when fully expressed, leads to growth & transformation

For further resources find us at: www.integraonline.org

You will find articles, movie lists, other resources on our website.

We'd love to hear from you, our readers. ***Please send us your comments & stories and your experience writing your way through your grief using this book.***

Watch for other versions of this book in different formats:
eBook, AudioBook, Study course

INTEGRA, P.O. Box 4005, East Lansing, MI 48826

More Grief Resources for You

Choose from among James E. Miller's popular books and DVDs on grief. Try out his newest electronic resource: *100 Healing Messages for Your Grief,* delivered via personalized email three times a week. Learn more at *www.willowgreen.com.*

10351 Dawson's Creek Blvd., Suite B / Fort Wayne IN 46825 / 260.490.2222

CPSIA information can be obtained
at www.ICGtesting.com
Printed in the USA
FFOW04n0155120418
46222907-47543FF

9 780977 298013